When I was young

by James Dunbar and Martin Remphry

W

FRANKLIN WATTS

NEW YORK•LONDON•SYDNEY

Josh likes visiting
Grandma Jenny.
Her apartment is full
of memories.

What was it like when you were young, Grandma? asked Josh.

And Grandma Jenny said –
When I was young...

50
years
ago

... we lived in
a new house.

I remember our first TV ...

We had a kitchen with an electric cooker and a fridge ...

Grandpa Ben used to visit us at weekends.

5

My sister used to dress up and go dancing every Saturday night.

Jenny remembered asking her Grandpa what it was like when he was young. Grandpa Ben sat Jenny on his knee and said –

When I was young...

100 years ago

My Mum and Dad worked in a big hotel. My Dad used to polish the carriages.

I saw a car in the street
for the first time.

Sometimes he let me
feed the horses.

9

I remember the first time we had our photo taken.

This is me in my sailor suit with Mum, Dad, brother Ted, sister May, Grandpa Jim and Grandma Emily.

Ben asked Grandma Emily what it was like when she was young.

150 years ago

Grandma Emily sat Ben on her knee and said –
When I was young...

I remember playing in the street with all the other children.

We lived in a busy town.
Grandpa used to take me
to the docks.

We watched the big ships come
and go from all around the world.

Emily used to ask her Grandpa
what it was like when he was young.

15

Grandpa Joe sat Emily on his knee and said –

When I was young…

200 years ago

I lived in the country. My Dad and Grandpa worked on a farm.

At harvest time everybody helped, even my Grandma Polly.

Two days each week we
went to the village school.

18

The teacher was very strict.

19

Joe remembered asking Grandma Polly what it was like when she was young. Grandma Polly sat Joe on her knee and said –

When I was young...

250 years ago

I used to help my older sister who worked at the big house.

Downstairs in the kitchen I polished candlesticks and scrubbed the tables and helped prepare the food.

Upstairs in the large rooms I dusted the furniture and helped make the fire.

I remember the fair coming to town.
There were games and dancing and
market stalls.

23

Polly used to ask her Grandpa what it was like when he was young...

300 years ago

Grandpa Will sat Polly on his knee and said –

When I was young...

We travelled to all the country markets where my dad and grandpa bought and sold horses.

I remember Grandma Betty making dolls and small toys. They were made from wood. I used to help paint the faces. She gave one of the wooden dolls to me ...

I remember thinking that when
I am as old as Grandma Betty,
I will tell my grandchildren
what it was like – when I was young.

Will, 1697
Polly's Grandpa

Joe, 1796
Emily's Grandpa

Betty, 1697
Will's Grandma

Polly, 1744
Joe's Grandma

Ben, 1899
Jenny's Grandpa

Josh, today

Emily, 1848
Ben's Grandma

Jenny, 1952
Josh's Grandma

Useful information

When Will was young ... in 1697 there were few shops, everything was bought and sold at the local market. Women sold things they had made at home and men would sell crops and vegetables they had grown, or animals they had bred.

When Polly was young ... in 1744 children started work as young as twelve. Boys might be grooms or stable boys and girls might work in kitchens or as maids. The fair would come to town about four times a year, on festival days.

When Joe was young ... in 1796 most families lived in the country. Children went to school about two days a week, and worked with their parents on the other days. Villages had only one teacher, and children wrote on a slate with chalk.

When Emily was young ... in 1848 it was the age of the machine. Families moved to the cities and worked in factories. Steamships and steam trains transported the factory-made goods. People lived in small homes with no running water.

When Ben was young ... in 1899 motor cars had just been invented. Cameras were still very large and complicated. Homes had gas lighting, and coal for heating. There were still no phones or electricity in the house.

When Jenny was young ... in 1952 not many people had a TV and programmes were in black and white. In their spare time people would listen to the radio or go out to the cinema or to dances. No-one had a computer at home, and space travel was still just a dream.

This edition 2014

First published by Franklin Watts,
338 Euston Road, London NW1 3BH

Franklin Watts Australia,
Level 17 / 207 Kent Street, Sydney NSW 2000

Text © 1999 James Dunbar
Illustrations © 1999 Martin Remphry
Notes and activities © 2004, 2014 Franklin Watts

Series editor: Paula Borton
Art director: Robert Walster

A CIP catalogue record is available from the British Library.
Dewey Classification 907

Printed in China

ISBN 978 1 4451 2896 2

Franklin Watts is a division of Hachette Children's Books,
an Hachette UK company. www.hachette.co.uk